SOPHOPHOBIA IS THE FEAR OF LEARNING

LEARN SOMETHING EVERYDAY

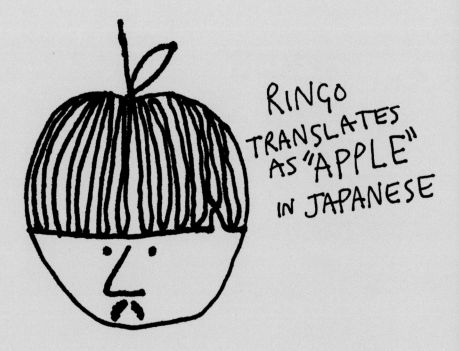

RINGO
TRANSLATES
AS "APPLE"
IN JAPANESE

LEARN SOMETHING EVERY DAY

YOUNG

A PERIGEE BOOK

A PERIGEE BOOK

PUBLISHED BY THE PENGUIN GROUP
PENGUIN GROUP (USA) INC.
375 HUDSON STREET, NEW YORK, NEW YORK 10014, USA

PENGUIN GROUP (CANADA), 90 EGLINTON AVENUE EAST, SUITE 700, TORONTO,
ONTARIO M4P 2Y3, CANADA (A DIVISION OF PEARSON PENGUIN CANADA INC.)
PENGUIN BOOKS LTD., 80 STRAND, LONDON WC2R ORL, ENGLAND
PENGUIN GROUP IRELAND, 25 ST. STEPHEN'S GREEN, DUBLIN 2, IRELAND
(A DIVISION OF PENGUIN BOOKS LTD.)
PENGUIN GROUP (AUSTRALIA), 250 CAMBERWELL ROAD, CAMBERWELL, VICTORIA 3124,
AUSTRALIA (A DIVISION OF PEARSON AUSTRALIA GROUP PTY. LTD.)
PENGUIN BOOKS INDIA PVT. LTD., 11 COMMUNITY CENTRE, PANCHSHEEL PARK,
NEW DELHI—110 017, INDIA
PENGUIN GROUP (NZ), 67 APOLLO DRIVE, ROSEDALE, NORTH SHORE 0632,
NEW ZEALAND (A DIVISION OF PEARSON NEW ZEALAND LTD.)
PENGUIN BOOKS (SOUTH AFRICA) (PTY.) LTD, 24 STURDEE AVENUE, ROSEBANK,
JOHANNESBURG 2196, SOUTH AFRICA
PENGUIN BOOKS LTD., REGISTERED OFFICES: 80 STRAND, LONDON WC2R ORL, ENGLAND

WHILE THE AUTHOR HAS MADE EVERY EFFORT TO PROVIDE ACCURATE TELEPHONE NUMBERS
AND INTERNET ADDRESSES AT THE TIME OF PUBLICATION, NEITHER THE PUBLISHER NOR THE
AUTHOR ASSUMES ANY RESPONSIBILITY FOR ERRORS OR FOR CHANGES THAT OCCUR
AFTER PUBLICATION. FURTHER, THE PUBLISHER DOES NOT HAVE ANY CONTROL OVER AND
DOES NOT ASSUME ANY RESPONSIBILITY FOR AUTHOR OR THIRD-PARTY WEBSITES OR THEIR CONTENT.

LEARN SOMETHING EVERY DAY

FIRST EDITION: MAY 2011
PERIGEE TRADE PAPERBACK ISBN: 978-0-399-53666-3

PRINTED IN THE UNITED STATES OF AMERICA
10 9 8 7 6 5 4

MOST PERIGEE BOOKS ARE AVAILABLE AT SPECIAL QUANTITY DISCOUNTS FOR BULK
PURCHASES FOR SALES PROMOTIONS, PREMIUMS, FUND-RAISING, OR EDUCATIONAL USE.
SPECIAL BOOKS, OR BOOK EXCERPTS, CAN ALSO BE CREATED TO FIT SPECIFIC NEEDS.
FOR DETAILS, WRITE: SPECIAL MARKETS, PENGUIN GROUP (USA) INC., 375 HUDSON STREET,
NEW YORK, NEW YORK 10014.

RIGHT-HANDED PEOPLE LIVE LONGER THAN LEFT-HANDED PEOPLE

CHARLIE CHAPLIN ONCE CAME IN THIRD IN A CHAPLIN LOOKALIKE CONTEST

CATS SLEEP FOR 70% OF THEIR LIVES

EMERSON MOSER,
CRAYOLA'S SENIOR
CRAYON
MAKER, REVEALED
AT RETIRÉMENT THAT
HE WAS COLOR-BLIND

Mind = blown!

ELEPHANTS
CAN'T
JUMP

DAVID BOWIE HAS A SPIDER SPECIES NAMED AFTER HIM

WAYNE ALLWINE, THE VOICE OF MICKEY MOUSE, WAS MARRIED TO RUSSI TAYLOR, THE VOICE OF MINNIE

Awww!

OWLS CAN'T MOVE THEIR EYES

THERE WAS NO
"MID SEPTEMBER"
IN 1752

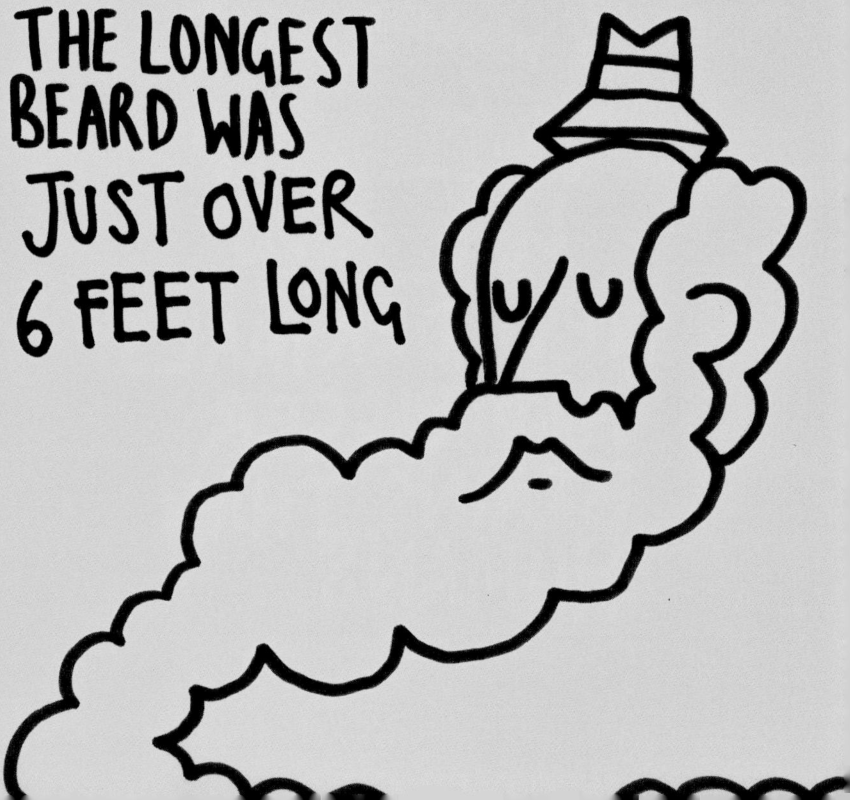
THE LONGEST BEARD WAS JUST OVER 6 FEET LONG

NEANDERTHALS
HAD BIGGER
BRAINS THAN
HUMANS

HUMANS SHARE ABOUT 50% OF DNA WITH BANANAS

THOMAS EDISON,
INVENTOR OF
THE LIGHTBULB,
WAS SCARED
OF THE DARK

STARFISH
HAVE NO
BRAINS

STAR PUPIL

JIM HENSON DEVELOPED AN ALLERGY TO FLEECE

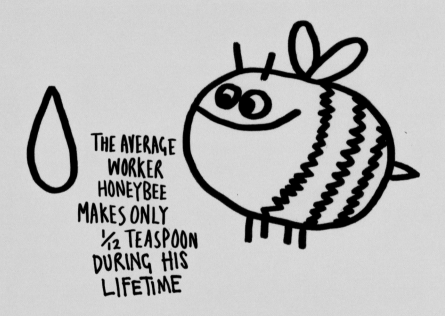

THE AVERAGE WORKER HONEYBEE MAKES ONLY 1/12 TEASPOON DURING HIS LIFETIME

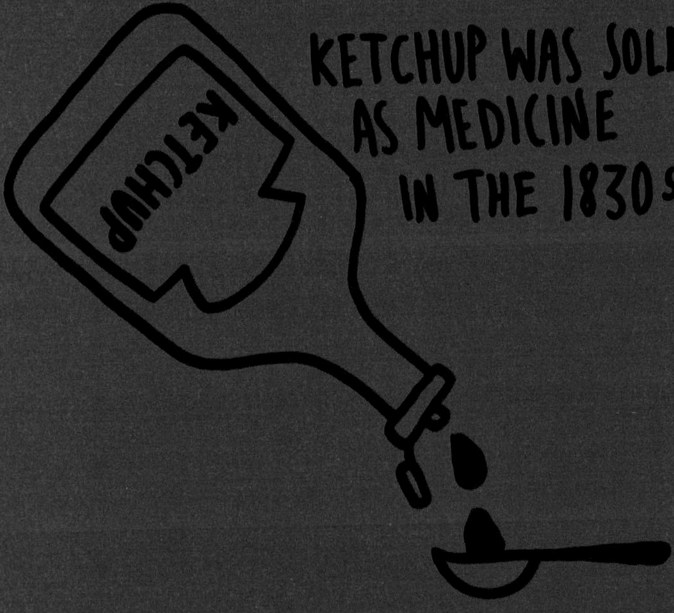

KETCHUP WAS SOLD AS MEDICINE IN THE 1830s

WOMEN CRY 4
TIMES AS OFTEN
AS MEN

That's cuz all the awesome
has to come out to prevent
buildup

JOHN LENNON'S CAT WAS CALLED ELVIS

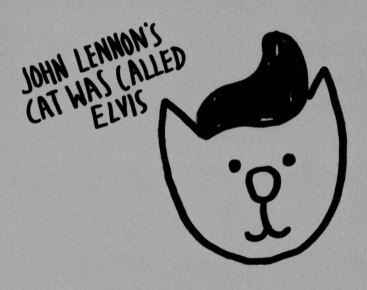

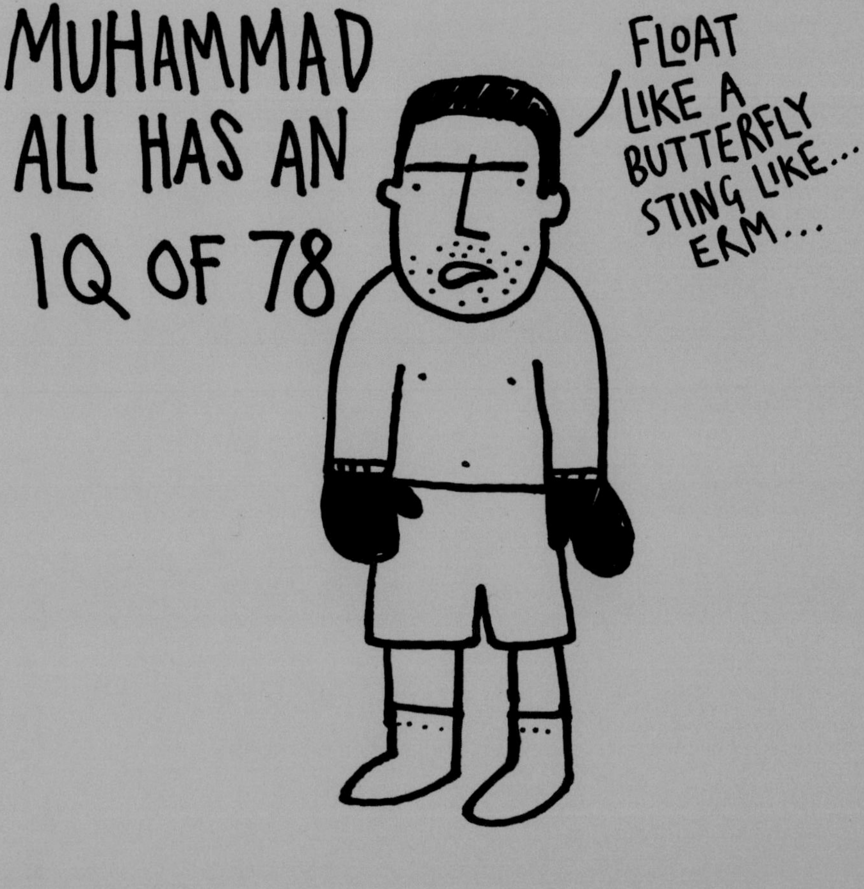
MUHAMMAD ALI HAS AN IQ OF 78
FLOAT LIKE A BUTTERFLY STING LIKE... ERM...

GOLF IS THE ONLY SPORT TO BE PLAYED ON THE MOON

4,000-YEAR-OLD CHEESE
WAS FOUND IN EGYPTIAN
TOMBS

130 CUPS OF TEA WOULD BE A LETHAL DOSE OF CAFFEINE

ESCAPIST
HARRY HOUDINI
DIED ON HALLOWEEN

HITLER WAS VOTED "TIME" MAGAZINE'S MAN OF THE YEAR IN 1938

SWEDISH SWEET MAKER ROLAND OHLSSON WAS BURIED IN A CHOCOLATE COFFIN

A DENTIST
INVENTED
THE ELECTRIC
CHAIR

ALL THE SWANS IN ENGLAND
ARE PROPERTY OF THE QUEEN

THE EAR

VAN GOGH ONLY
SOLD ONE PAINTING
DURING HIS
LIFETIME

ANTS CAN LIFT
50 TIMES
THEIR WEIGHT

THE FATTEST MAN WAS 1,400 POUNDS

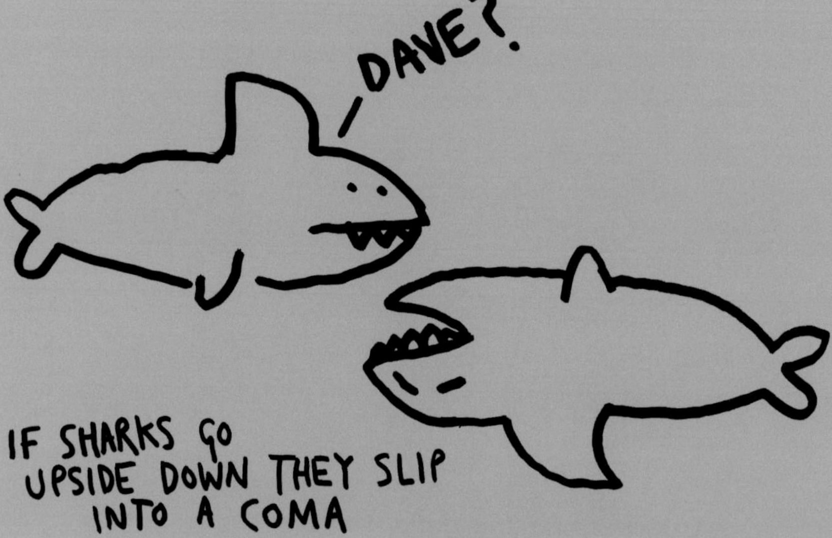
DAVE?
IF SHARKS GO UPSIDE DOWN THEY SLIP INTO A COMA

A HERD OF GIRAFFES IS CALLED A TOWER

BARRY MANILOW DIDN'T WRITE HIS HIT "I WRITE THE SONGS"

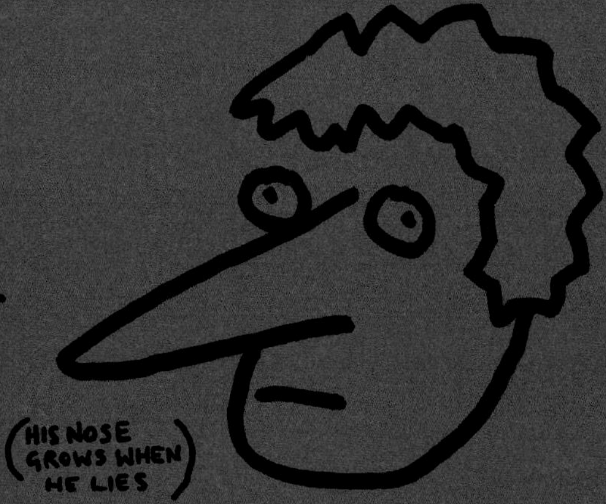

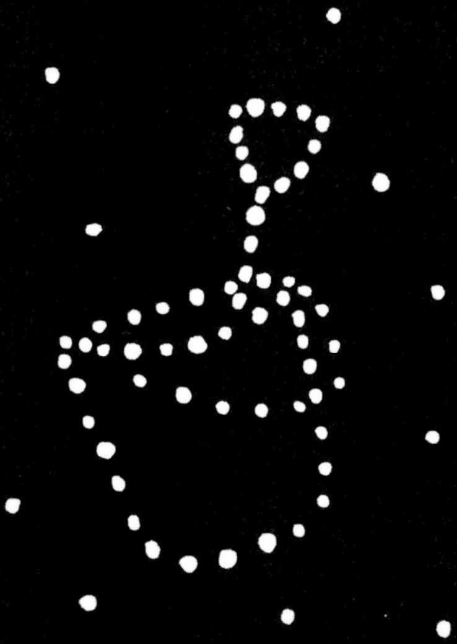

THERE ARE MORE
STARS IN THE SKY
THAN GRAINS OF
SAND ON THE EARTH

THE SPACE BETWEEN YOUR
EYEBROWS IS CALLED THE GLABELLA

EARTHWORMS HAVE UP TO 9 HEARTS

ABBA NEVER USED THE ABBA
RHYMING PATTERN

BATS
ALWAYS
TURN LEFT
WHEN EXITING
A CAVE

THE BEATLES USED THE WORD "LOVE" 613 TIMES IN THEIR SONGS

THE AVERAGE PERSON RELOCATES
11 TIMES

THE ONLY GUY WITHOUT A
BEARD IN ZZ TOP
HAS THE
SURNAME
BEARD

THERE ARE
AROUND 61
TREES PER PERSON

THE SMALLEST
BONE IN YOUR BODY
IS IN YOUR EAR

COLUMBUS
BELIEVED THE
EARTH WAS
PEAR SHAPED

CATS
CAN'T TASTE
SWEETNESS

poor kitties!

GOLDFISH CAN'T
CLOSE THEIR EYES

CHILDREN GROW FASTER DURING SPRING

Thank goodness for capris!

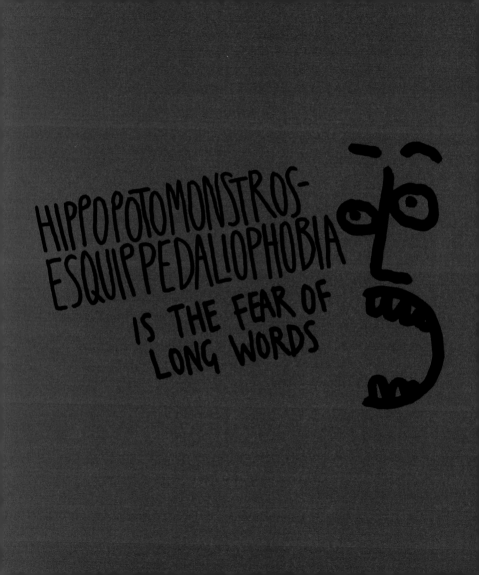

THE AVERAGE
HUMAN BODY
CONTAINS
ENOUGH IRON
TO MAKE A
3-INCH NAIL

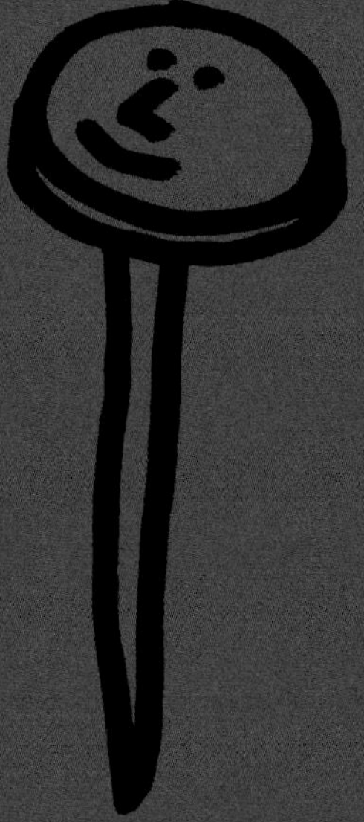

BARBIE'S FULL NAME
IS BARBARA MILLICENT
ROBERTS

THOU SHALT NOT STEAL

THE BIBLE IS THE MOST SHOPLIFTED BOOK

Irony?

A RUBIK'S CUBE HAS
43,252,003,274,489,856,000
POSSIBLE COMBINATIONS

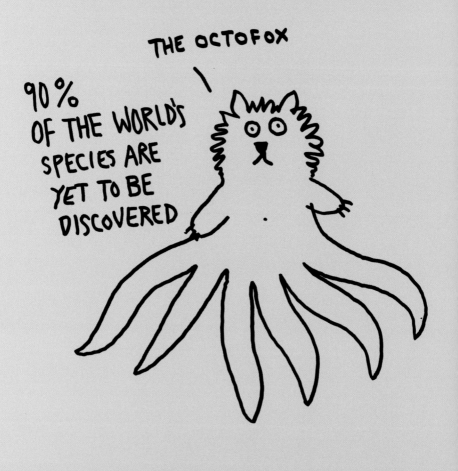

TENNIS PLAYER
VIKTOR TROICKI
IS ALLERGIC TO GRASS

THE SLOWEST
FISH IS
A SEAHORSE

LOU REED WAS GIVEN
ELECTROSHOCK TREATMENT
WHEN HE WAS YOUNG

BABOONS WERE
ONCE TRAINED
BY EGYPTIANS
TO WAIT ON
TABLES

I think I've worked
with a few :

GIRAFFES CLEAN THEIR EARS WITH THEIR 18-INCH-LONG TONGUES

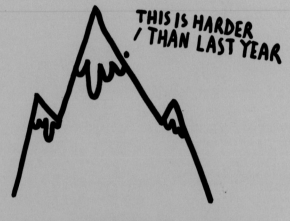

THIS IS HARDER
/ THAN LAST YEAR

MOUNT EVEREST GROWS
1/4 INCH A YEAR

ON
AVERAGE,
WOMEN
LIVE LONGER
THAN MEN

TO LIFT A 110 POUND PERSON, YOU'LL NEED 4,000 HELIUM BALLOONS

MEN ARE
MORE LIKELY
TO GET
STRUCK BY
LIGHTNING
THAN WOMEN

ANCIENT
EGYPTIANS
THOUGHT
HEDGEHOGS CURED
BALDNESS

THE LONGEST BOXING MATCH LASTED 110 ROUNDS

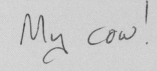

STAYING
AWAKE
FOR 2 WEEKS
CAN KILL
YOU

THE KING
OF HEARTS
IS THE ONLY
KING WITHOUT
A MUSTACHE

THE "MONA LISA" HAS NO EYEBROWS

ADULT FEET
PRODUCE
1/4 CUP
OF SWEAT
A DAY

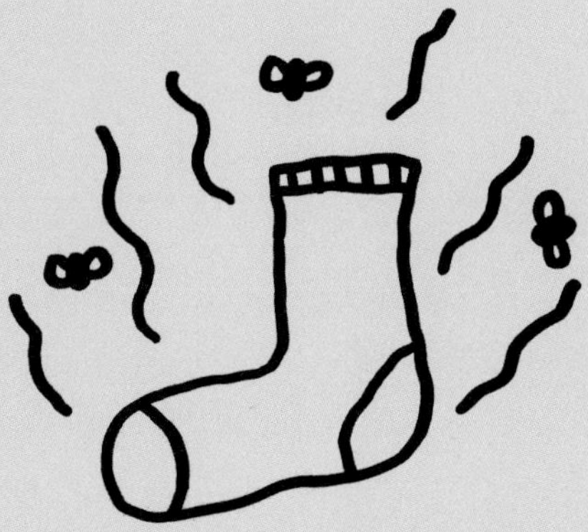

Um... ew!

ONE CIGARETTE TAKES 5 MINUTES OFF THE SMOKER'S LIFE

95% OF PEOPLE CAN
GUESS SOMEONE'S SEX
JUST FROM SMELLING
THEIR BREATH

A BEAVER'S TEETH NEVER STOP GROWING

Nor do rabbit's or hamster's.

14.4 MILLION LETTERS ARE LOST IN THE MAIL EACH YEAR

FERRETS CAN SUFFER FROM DEPRESSION

A DOG'S
SENSE OF SMELL
IS 100 TIMES AS GOOD
AS A HUMAN'S

ROARING SCHOOL

CHEETAHS
CAN'T
ROAR

WALRUSES HAVE 3 TIMES THE SUCKING POWER OF A VACUUM CLEANER

Who tests this?!?

YOU CAN WALK ON CUSTARD

MORE MEN THAN WOMEN
TAKE TEDDY BEARS TO BED

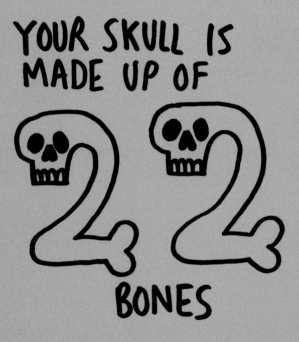

NEWBORN BABIES
BLINK ONLY
ONCE OR TWICE
A MINUTE

THE HORMONE THAT MAKES
YOU GROW IS PRODUCED ONLY
WHEN YOU SLEEP

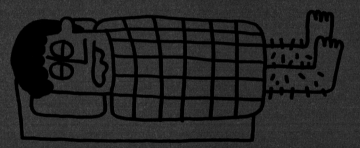

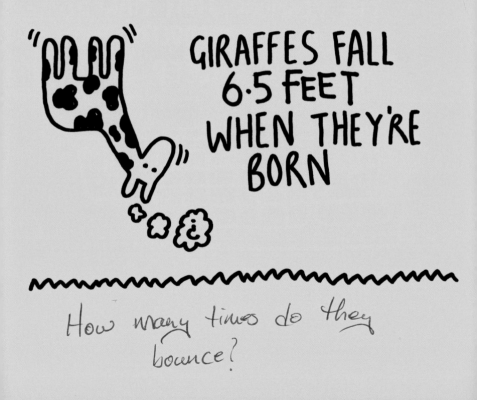

GIRAFFES FALL 6·5 FEET WHEN THEY'RE BORN

How many times do they bounce?

HUMANS ARE THE ONLY ANIMALS THAT CRY TEARS WHEN SAD

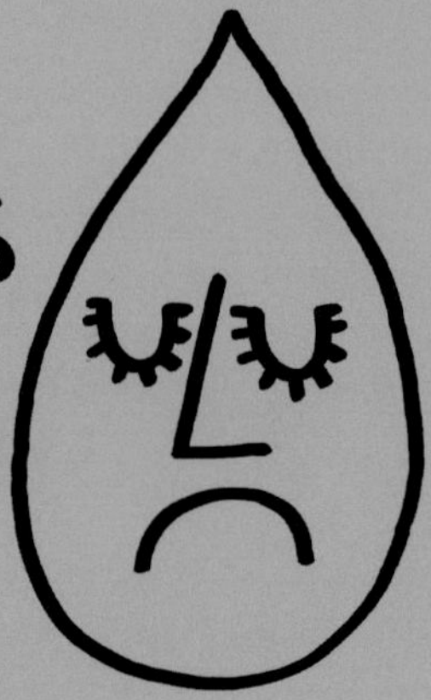

THERE IS
NO SUNSHINE
IN THE
SOUTH POLE
FOR 182 DAYS
A YEAR

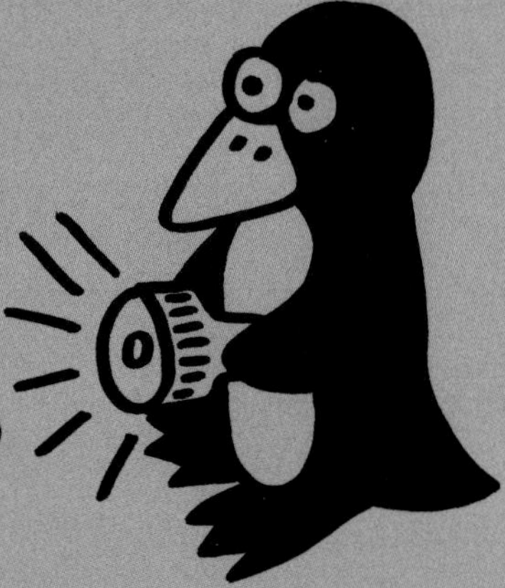

THE OLDEST
PERSON TO
GROW A TOOTH
WAS 125 YEARS
OLD

SCIENTISTS HAVE INVENTED GLOW-IN-THE-DARK PIGS

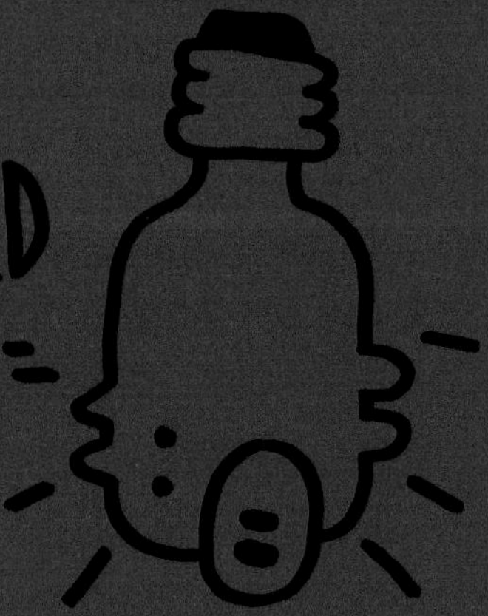

Why?

A MOUSE'S
HEART BEATS
EVERY 0.009
SECONDS

A FLASH OF LIGHTNING TAKES 0.0001 SECONDS

ANTEATERS
CAN EAT
UP TO 30,000
ANTS A DAY

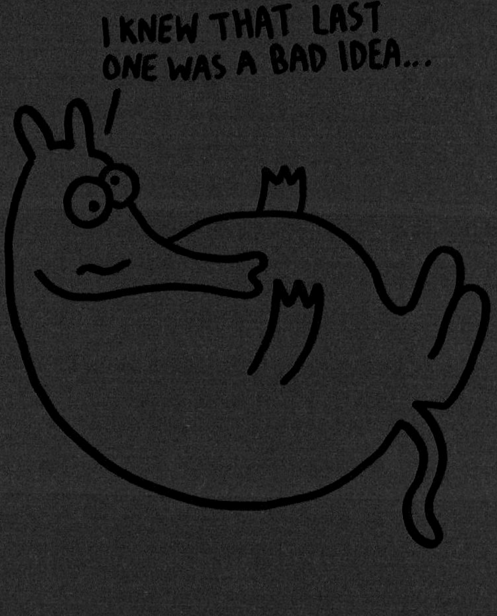

THERE'S ENOUGH CARBON IN YOUR BODY TO MAKE 900 PENCILS

THE AVERAGE
HEAD GROWS
115 FEET OF
HAIR A DAY

ABOVE AVERAGE

BELOW AVERAGE

WOMEN'S PUBLIC
BATHROOMS CONTAIN
TWICE AS MUCH
BACTERIA
THAN MEN'S

Um... EW!!

IN MOST HOMES, THE TOILET CONTAINS FEWER GERMS THAN THE KITCHEN

ON AVERAGE,
12 NEWBORNS
WILL BE GIVEN
TO THE WRONG
PARENTS
EVERY DAY

What!!?!

FLIES EAT BY VOMITING ON THEIR FOOD

ON AVERAGE, A HAMSTER WILL RUN UP TO 3 MILES A NIGHT

Go, Chester, go!!

A CAT WOULD
HAVE TO EAT 5
MICE TO GAIN
THE SAME
NUTRITIONAL
VALUE AS A CAN
OF CAT FOOD

 = ?

EINSTEIN COULD NEVER
REMEMBER HIS PHONE
NUMBER

SHAKESPEARE
WAS DYSLEXIC

REMEO & JULEIT

"SPACE INVADERS" WAS SO POPULAR IN JAPAN IT CREATED A COIN SHORTAGE

DOGS LIKE EATING
CAT POO

YOU CAN
MAKE DIAMONDS
OUT OF DEAD
PEOPLE

THE MOST HATED SOUND
IS THAT OF SOMEONE VOMITING

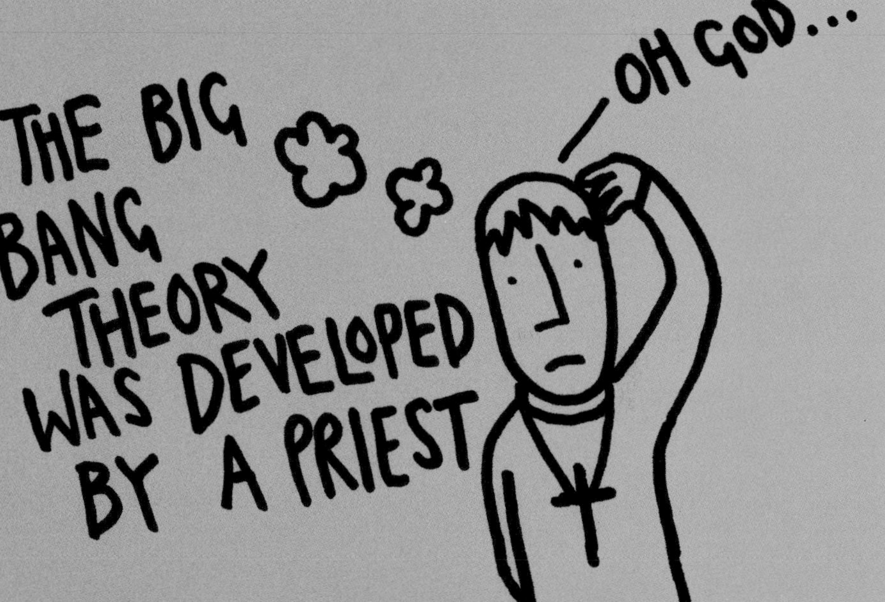
THE BIG BANG THEORY WAS DEVELOPED BY A PRIEST
OH GOD...

THE WOLF
SPIDER
CARRIES ITS
YOUNG ON
ITS BACK

TOXOCARA WORMS
CAN EAT THROUGH
A HUMAN EYEBALL

THERE ARE MORE THAN 600 SPECIES OF CARNIVOROUS PLANTS

ANCIENT GREEKS BELIEVED THAT PIGEON DROPPINGS STIMULATED HAIR GROWTH

HOWARD HUGHES'S
TOENAILS GREW
TO ALMOST
6 INCHES LONG

THE WORM BEE

AROUND 10,000 NEW INSECTS ARE DISCOVERED EVERY YEAR

AN ADULT MAN'S BODY CONTAINS 1·5 GALLONS OF BLOOD

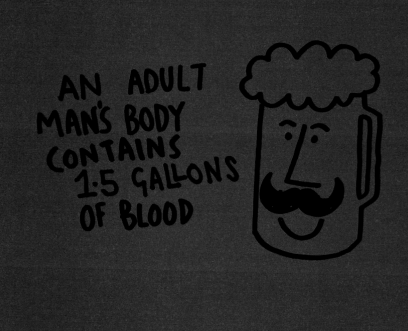

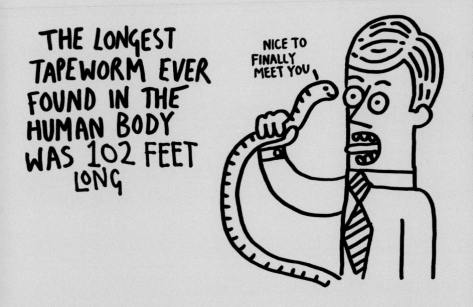

WOODPECKERS
SLAM THEIR
HEADS INTO TREES
AT A RATE OF
20 PECKS A SECOND

THE LARGEST KNOWN FROG IS THE GOLIATH FROG, MEASURING UP TO 34.5 INCHES LONG

THE CANADIAN
COCKTAIL SOURTOE
CONTAINS A PRESERVED
HUMAN TOE

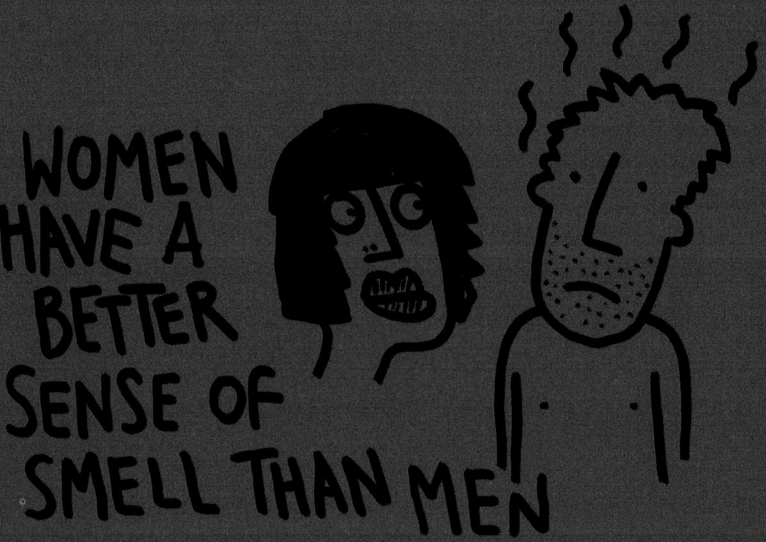
WOMEN HAVE A BETTER SENSE OF SMELL THAN MEN

STUNTMAN
EVEL
KNIEVEL
HOLDS THE
RECORD
FOR THE
MOST BROKEN
BONES - 35

STANDING FOR AN HOUR BURNS 120 CALORIES

YOUR SENSE OF HEARING IS AT ITS BEST AT 10 YEARS OLD

SOME PERFUMES
CONTAIN WHALE
VOMIT

GEORGE W. BUSH WAS A SCHOOL CHEERLEADER

MORE THAN 67% OF AMERICANS ARE CONSIDERED OVERWEIGHT

THE OLDEST
LIVING TREE
IS 10,000
YEARS OLD

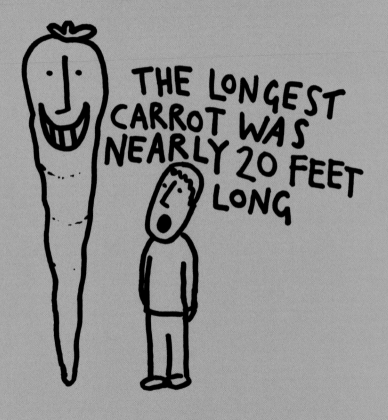

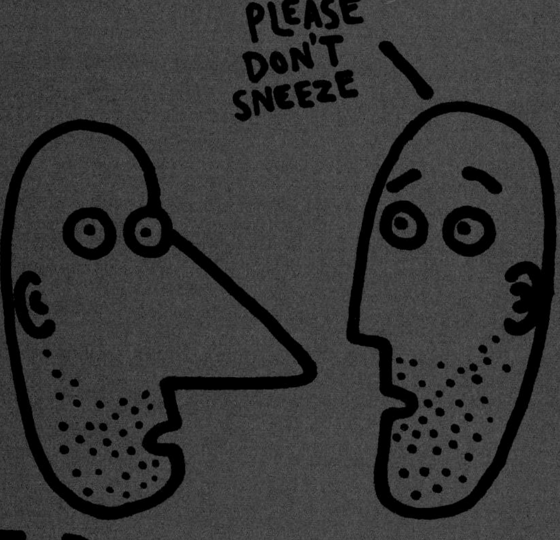

THE BIGGEST NOSE WAS 17.5 INCHES LONG

SHARKS
HAVE THE
BEST SENSE
OF SMELL
OF ANYFISH

THE FIRST EMAIL
MESSAGE WAS

QWERTYUIOP

THE FIRST LIVING
EARTHLING IN
SPACE WAS A DOG

FRANCE
IS THE MOST
POPULAR TOURIST
DESTINATION

THE FIRST
MAN TO HAVE
FLOWN WAS
FRENCH

THE LONGEST MUSTACHE WAS 11.5 FEET LONG

AN ALBATROSS CAN
FLY NONSTOP
FOR 10 YEARS

Wow

THE LAST
DODO
DIED IN
1681

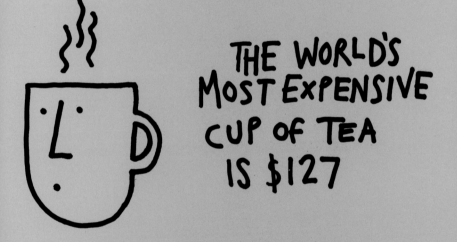

THE WORLD'S MOST EXPENSIVE CUP OF TEA IS $127

HENRY VIII TECHNICALLY HAD 2 WIVES NOT 6

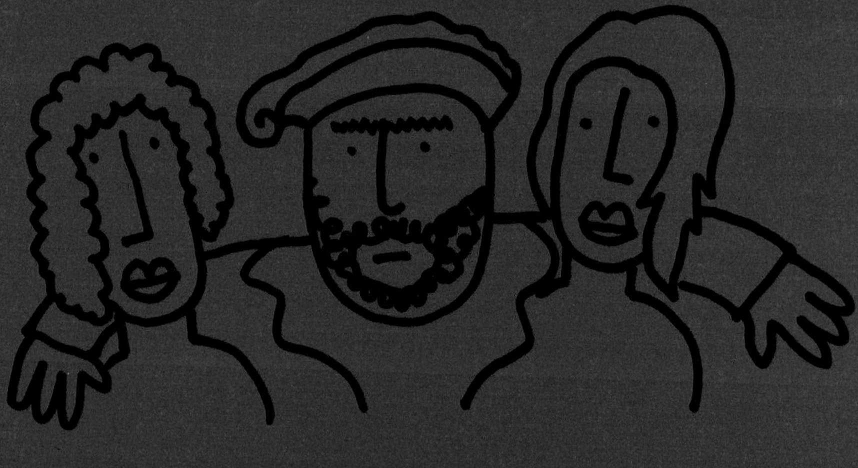

BASEBALL WAS INVENTED IN ENGLAND

THE TALLEST CAKE WAS 108 FEET TALL

HELP

THE FIRST COMPUTER BUG WAS A REAL BUG

THE LONGEST
BEARD ON A
WOMAN WAS
14 INCHES
LONG

THE BEACH BOYS' DENNIS WILSON DROWNED

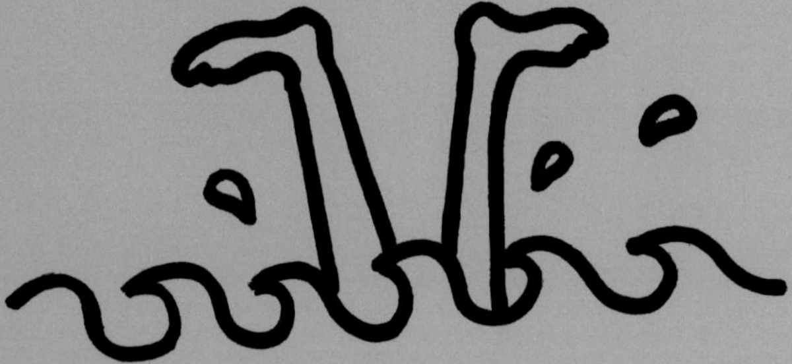

THE LOUDEST BURP WAS 107.1 dB (AS LOUD AS A CHAINSAW)

Nice!

THE WORLD'S OLDEST MAN WAS 138

HAPPY
BIRTHDAY
GREAT
GREAT
GREAT
GRANDAD

PICASSO'S FULL NAME WAS:
PABLO DIEGO JOSÉ FRANCISCO
DE PAULA JUAN NEPOMUCENO
MARÍA DE LOS REMEDIOS
CIPRIANO DE LA SANTISIMA
TRINIDAD RUIZ Y PICASSO

THE FASTEST
A HUMAN
MOVED
24,791
MILES
AN HOUR

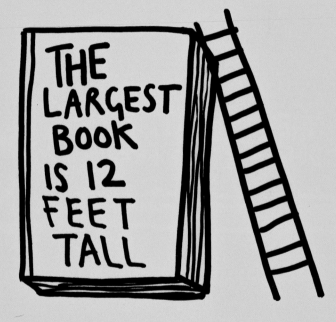

THE MOST EXPENSIVE CAR LICENSE PLATE IS

THE NUMBER ONE

THE
TALLEST
MAN
EVER
WAS
NEARLY
9 FEET
TALL

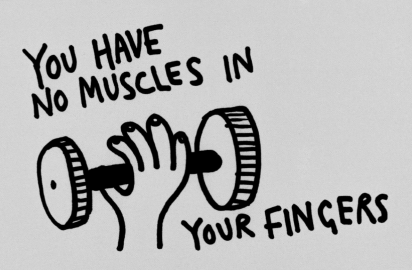

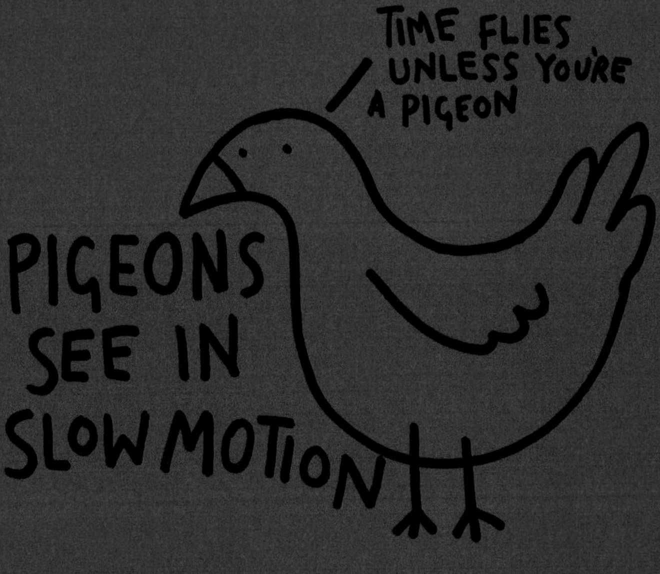
TIME FLIES UNLESS YOU'RE A PIGEON
PIGEONS SEE IN SLOW MOTION

RATS
EAT 20% OF
THE WORLD'S
FOOD
SUPPLY

Pigs.

THE CARNIVOROUS POLAR BEAR LOVES TOOTHPASTE

THE WORLD'S
OLDEST
BUNGEE
JUMPER WAS
83

A HIPPO HAS THE LARGEST MOUTH OF ALL LAND ANIMALS

THE MOST PEOPLE
CRAMMED INTO A
MINI IS 21

THERE ARE
TWICE AS
MANY PEOPLE
ALIVE TODAY
AS IN
1960

STOP STARING AT ME

A CHAMELEON'S CHANGING COLOR ISN'T CAMOUFLAGE— IT'S COMMUNICATION

THE DEADLIEST SPIDER IS THE BANANA SPIDER

Seen one of those... scary!

THE HIGHEST
WAVE ON
RECORD IS
1,719 FEET
HIGH

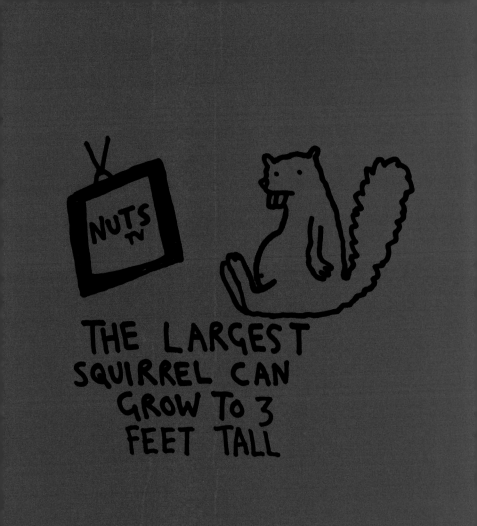

THE LARGEST
SQUIRREL CAN
GROW TO 3
FEET TALL

ROMANS WHO
DISCOVERED
PARROTS TAUGHT
THEM TO SAY
"HAIL CAESAR!"

SSSSSSSUNBATHE

SNAKES ARE AVID.
SUN BATHERS

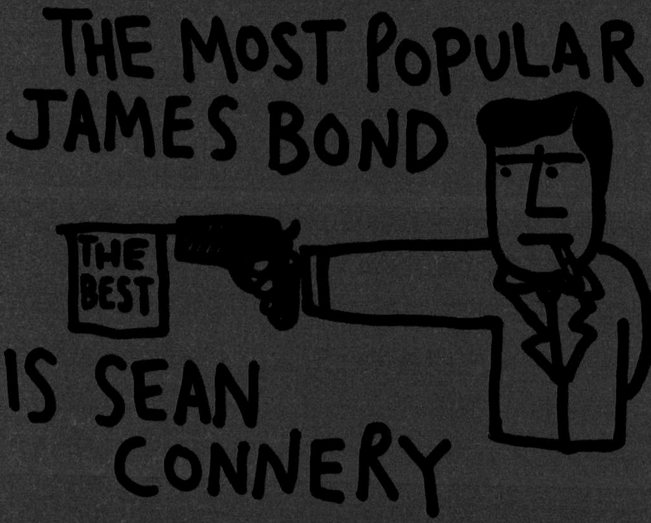
THE MOST POPULAR
JAMES BOND
THE BEST
IS SEAN
CONNERY

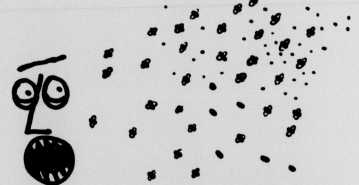

2 FLIES CAN PRODUCE
191,010,000,000,000,000,000
OFFSPRING IN 4 MONTHS

A LION'S LIFE
EXPECTANCY IS SHORTER
THAN THE ANTELOPE
IT CHASES

HORSES CAN SLEEP STANDING UP

HAPPY 255TH

THE OLDEST CREATURE
WAS A 255-YEAR-
OLD TORTOISE

THERE ARE MORE WORMS IN THE WORLD THAN ANY OTHER CREATURE

LOVE MOBILE

A WHALE'S HEART
IS AS BIG AS A CAR

OSCAR WILDE'S
LAST WORDS WERE
"EITHER THE WALLPAPER
GOES OR I DO"

CHOCOLATE IS POISONOUS TO PARROTS

THE AVERAGE
BEEHIVE HAS
40-45,000
BEES INSIDE

THE FIRST
5 TARZAN
FILMS WERE
SILENT

AAAAAAH!

THE LIGHT
OF 6 LARGE
FIREFLIES
IS ENOUGH
TO READ BY

Cool

STRAWBERRIES CONTAIN MORE VITAMIN C THAN ORANGES

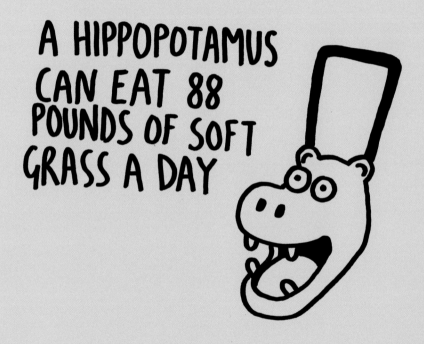

A HIPPOPOTAMUS CAN EAT 88 POUNDS OF SOFT GRASS A DAY

THE CALL OF A BLUE
WHALE IS LOUDER THAN
A JUMBO JET

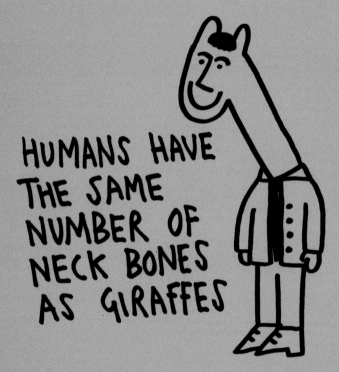

HUMANS HAVE
THE SAME
NUMBER OF
NECK BONES
AS GIRAFFES

A SINGLE STRAND OF HAIR CAN STAY ON YOUR HEAD FOR 5 YEARS

85% OF PEOPLE CAN CURL THEIR TONGUE

EATING
RED PEPPERS
TURNS
CANARIES
ORANGE

Ok, that's a little weird.

THE QUEEN
OF ENGLAND
OWNS A
RUBBER DUCK
WEARING A
CROWN

75% OF PEOPLE WEAR THE WRONG SIZE SHOES

THERE ARE AN ESTIMATED

3,510

VARIATIONS OF CHILI PEPPERS

THE OLDEST GOLDFISH WAS 43

DEER HAVE
INFRARED
VISION

EATING 2·2 POUNDS OF POTATOES IN ONE SITTING WILL KILL YOU

Again ... who measures this?

A BASKETBALL-SIZED OCTOPUS CAN FIT INTO A SODA CAN

THE HEAVIEST
CAT WEIGHED
47 POUNDS

INSECT
BLOOD
IS YELLOW

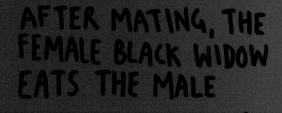

YOU ARE MORE LIKELY TO BE KILLED BY AN ASTEROID THAN BY LIGHTNING

Comforting?

BEETHOVEN WAS ONCE ARRESTED FOR LOOKING LIKE A TRAMP

A BABY ROBIN
EATS AROUND
13 FEET OF
EARTHWORMS
A DAY

IN 2007,
A 4-LEGGED
DUCK WAS
BORN

BEN & JERRY'S ICE CREAM WASTE IS FED TO PIGS

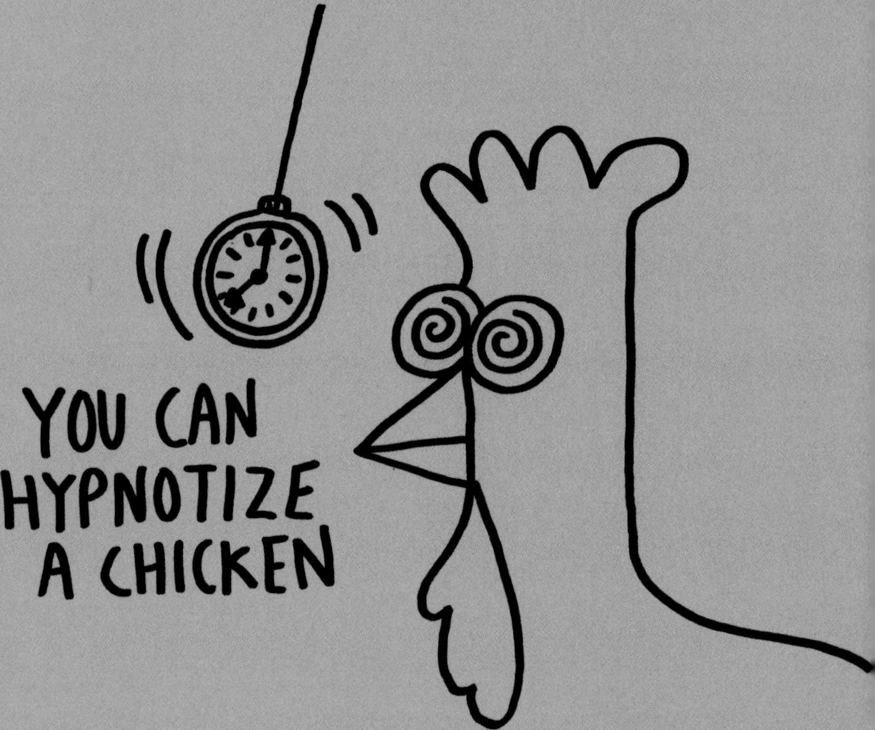
YOU CAN
HYPNOTIZE
A CHICKEN

THE WETTEST
PLACE ON EARTH IS THE
INDIAN TOWN CHERRAPUNJI

THE PLASTIC
BIT AT THE END
OF SHOELACES IS
CALLED AN AGLET

FISH CAN DROWN

BEETLES DON'T LIKE
HEAVY METAL MUSIC

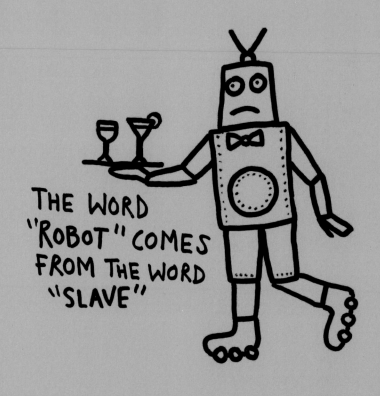

THE WORD
"ROBOT" COMES
FROM THE WORD
"SLAVE"

THE SUN IS
4·5 BILLION
YEARS OLD

A HUGELY
INACCURATE
"DAILY
MIRROR"
HEADLINE
READ...

DAILY MIRROR©

TITANIC
SUNK—
NO LIVES
LOST

RUSSIAN TREE DOLLS

A QUARTER OF ALL FORESTS ARE IN RUSSIA

THE RECORD FOR HOLDING THE BREATH UNDER WATER IS 9 MINUTES, 8 SECONDS

THE FIRST
ROBOT WAS
A DUCK

IF YOU WEE
IN THE SHOWER
INSTEAD OF
FLUSHING A
TOILET, YOU COULD
SAVE 1,157
GALLONS OF WATER
A YEAR

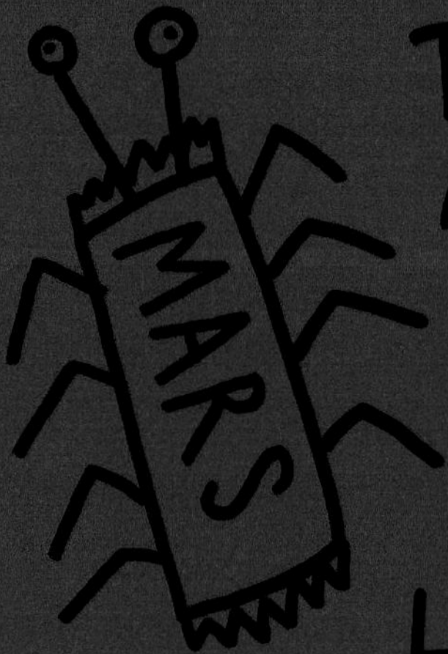

THE AVERAGE CHOCOLATE BAR HAS 8 INSECT LEGS IN IT

A BOLT OF LIGHTNING HAS ENOUGH ENERGY TO TOAST 160,000 PIECES OF BREAD

THE HAPPY BIRTHDAY SONG IS COPYRIGHTED TILL 2030
YOU OWE MONEY
HAPPY BIRTHDAY TO ME...

HULK
HOGAN'S
REAL
NAME IS
TERRY

ROMANS USED TO CLEAN THEIR TEETH WITH...

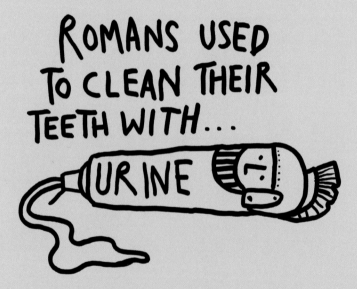

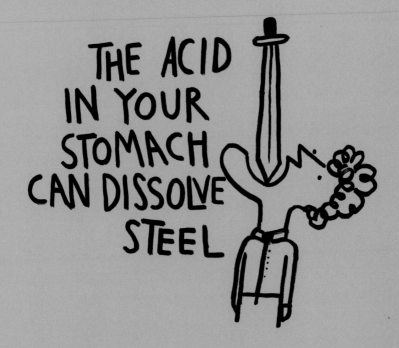

OYSTERS CAN
CHANGE GENDER

ANTS HAVE THE BIGGEST BRAINS IN PROPORTION TO THEIR BODIES

IN 1314,
KING
EDWARD II
BANNED
SOCCER
IN ENGLAND

ORIGINALLY BRIDES CARRIED WEDDING FLOWERS TO MASK BODY ODOR

MONDAY THE 27TH IS STATISTICALLY MORE UNLUCKY THAN FRIDAY THE 13TH

FLIES BEAT THEIR WINGS 180 TIMES A SECOND

RIP DAVE

AROUND 250 PEOPLE HAVE DIED AFTER FALLING FROM THE LEANING TOWER OF PISA

BEING CRUSHED
BY AN ELEPHANT
WAS A POPULAR
FORM OF
EXECUTION IN
ASIA

THE MOST POWERFUL MUSCLE IN YOUR BODY IS USED FOR CHEWING

THE LOUDEST SNORE
RECORDED WAS 93 DECIBELS—
LOUDER THAN A CAR ENGINE

3,000-YEAR-OLD MUMMIES STILL HAVE THEIR FINGER-PRINTS

THE LARGEST
LIVING THING
IS A MUSHROOM

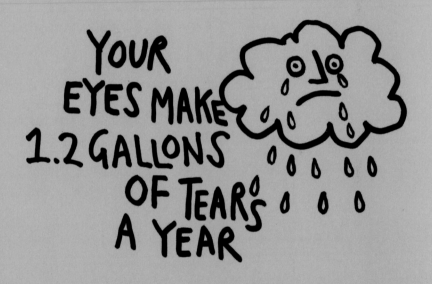

THERE'S MORE BACTERIA IN YOUR MOUTH THAN THERE ARE PEOPLE IN THE WORLD

IN 1740, A COW WAS ACCUSED OF BEING A WITCH AND KILLED

RUDOLPH THE REINDEER IS A FEMALE

IF YOU MULTIPLY
111,111,111
BY
111,111,111
YOU GET
12,345,678,987,654,321

KING LOUIS XVI, VICTIM OF THE GUILLOTINE, HELPED DESIGN IT

"STAR TREK" CREATOR GENE RODDENBERRY HAD THE FIRST SPACE FUNERAL

SPANISH IS MORE WIDELY SPOKEN THAN ENGLISH

AN ANAGRAM OF ALBERT EINSTEIN IS TEN ELITE BRAINS

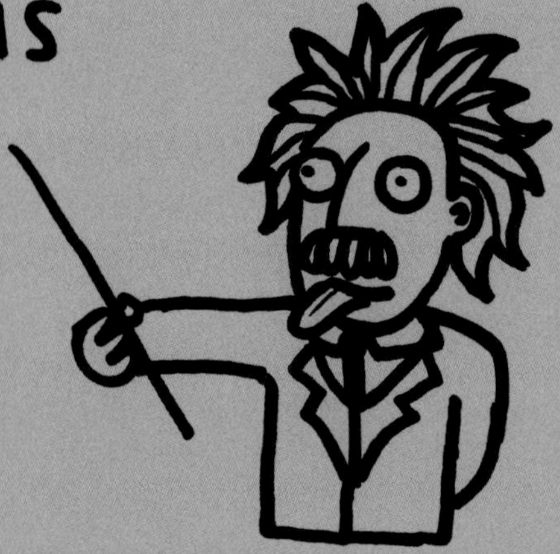

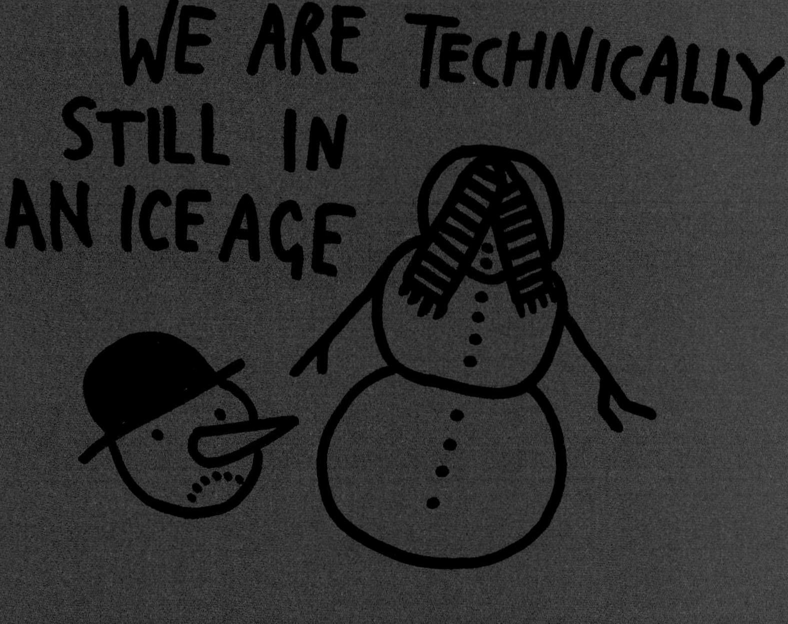
WE ARE TECHNICALLY STILL IN AN ICE AGE

BUTTERFLIES HAVE GREAT HEARING

THERE ARE
3 TOWNS IN
AMERICA
CALLED
SANTA CLAUS

WELCOME TO
SANTA CLAUS

THE WORLD'S LONGEST
RUNNING PLAY IS
"MOUSETRAP"

THE FIRST
WORD RECORDED
WAS "MARY"

MARY HAD A
LITTLE LAMB

45 RPM

AND MANY
MORE

NEW YORK USED TO BE CALLED NEW AMSTERDAM

THERE IS NO SUCH
NUMBER AS A ZILLION

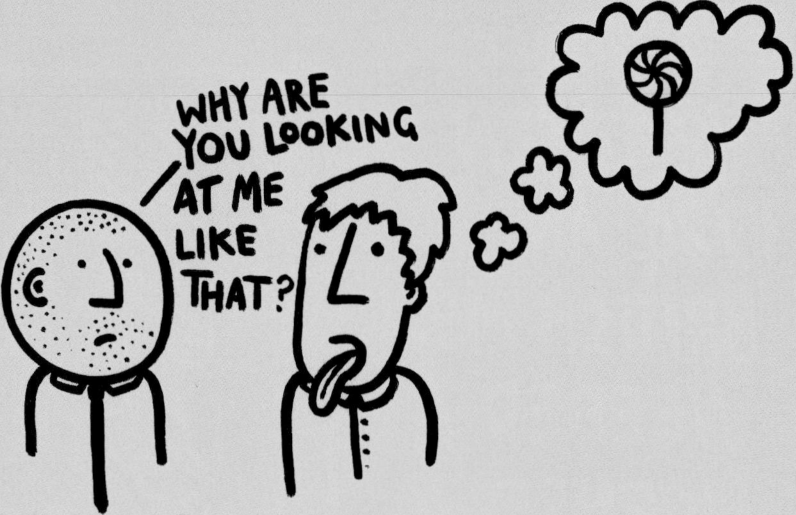

SUGAR IS THE ONLY TASTE HUMANS ARE BORN CRAVING

BETWEEN 1784 AND 1811, BRITISH MEN NEEDED A LICENSE TO WEAR A HAT

WANTED:
WITH OR WITHOUT HAT

PICASSO
WAS ONCE
ACCUSED OF
STEALING
THE "MONA LISA"

PICASSO'S
VERSION

THERE ARE MORE SHEEP IN THE BIBLE THAN ANY OTHER ANIMAL

THE BIBLE

Baah!

MOZART
BEGAN
COMPOSING
AT AGE 5

THE
RECORD
FOR SNEEZING
IS 2.5
YEARS

Bless you!

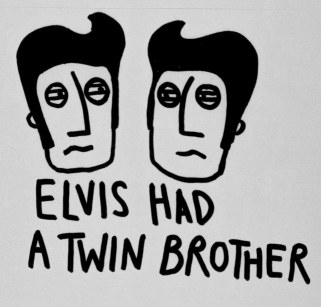

ELVIS HAD
A TWIN BROTHER

HARD WORK

VITUS IS THE PATRON SAINT OF DOG BITES

URUGUAY USED HARD CHEESE AS CANNON-BALLS IN A WAR WITH BRAZIL

THE
STATUE
OF LIBERTY
WAS MADE
IN FRANCE

TV SOAP OPERAS
ARE SO CALLED
BECAUSE THEY
WERE SPONSORED
BY SOAP
MANUFACTURERS

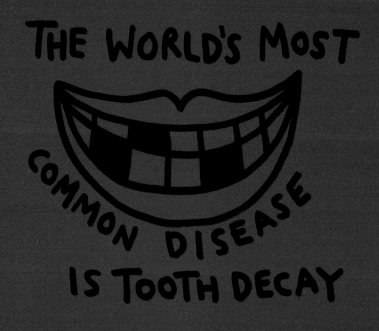

THE WORLD'S MOST COMMON DISEASE IS TOOTH DECAY

A FEMALE ELEPHANT
IS CALLED A COW

That's not nice,
she's big-boned!

THE FIRST SONG VIDEO ON MTV WAS "VIDEO KILLED THE RADIO STAR"

THE ENGLISH INVENTED CHAMPAGNE

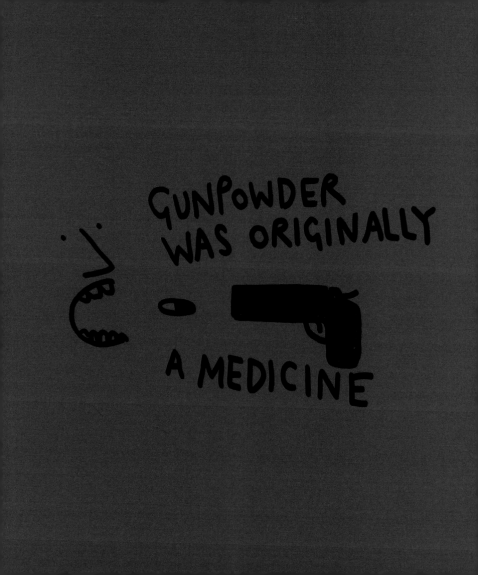

← 9 LIVES

CATS CAN SURVIVE
FALLS FROM ABOVE
THE 7TH FLOOR OF
BUILDINGS

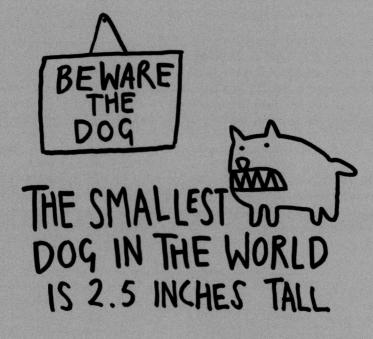

GEORGE WASHINGTON
HAD FALSE TEETH
MADE FROM
HIPPO TEETH

A DAY ISN'T
EXACTLY
24 HOURS
LONG

CHARLIE CHAPLIN'S CORPSE WAS ONCE STOLEN

THE MONTH
OF JULY WAS
NAMED AFTER
JULIUS
CAESAR

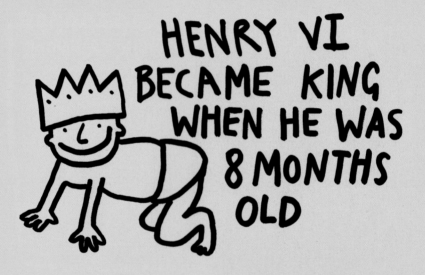

HENRY VI BECAME KING WHEN HE WAS 8 MONTHS OLD

THE FASTEST CREATURE IS A FALCON, REACHING 185 MPH

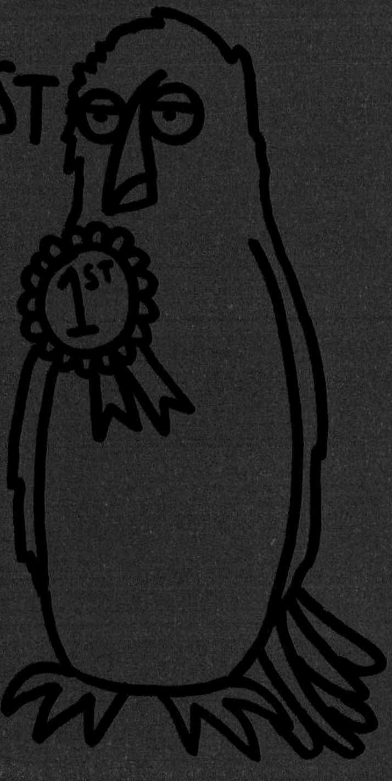

ON AVERAGE
BRITONS EAT
11 POUNDS OF
BAKED BEANS
A YEAR

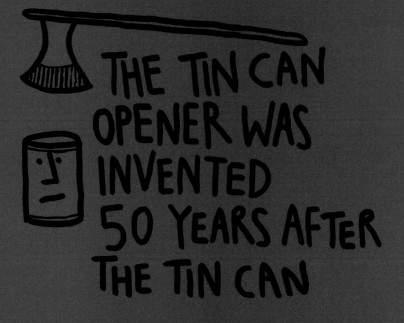

THE TIN CAN
OPENER WAS
INVENTED
50 YEARS AFTER
THE TIN CAN

80% OF IMAGES ON THE INTERNET ARE PORNOGRAPHIC

NOT THIS ONE

MOST SPIDERS
HAVE 8 EYES

Really didn't need
to know this

THERE ARE
NO CLOCKS
IN LAS VEGAS
CASINOS

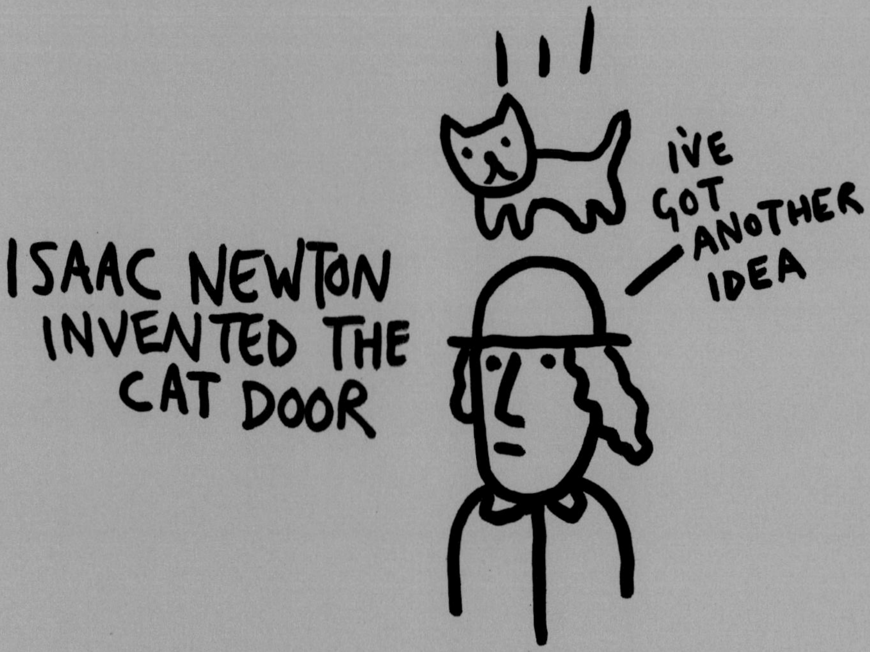
ISAAC NEWTON INVENTED THE CAT DOOR
IVE GOT ANOTHER IDEA

IF YOU RECEIVED ALL OF THE GIFTS
IN THE SONG "12 DAYS OF CHRISTMAS"
YOU WOULD RECEIVE 364 PRESENTS

THE LARGEST MAN-MADE STRUCTURE IS A TRASH DUMP IN NEW YORK

THE WORLD'S OLDEST LIGHTBULB HASN'T BEEN TURNED OFF SINCE 1901

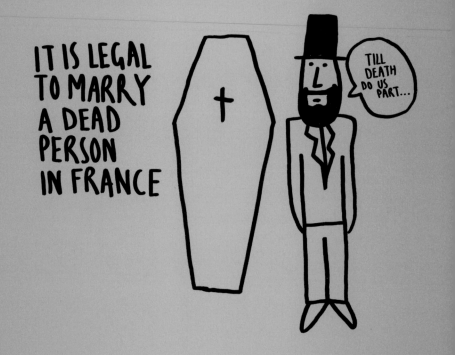

THE AVERAGE PENCIL CAN
DRAW A 35-MILE-LONG LINE

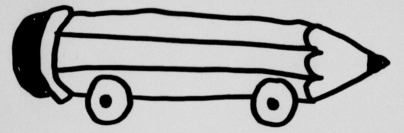

ALEXANDER GRAHAM
BELL, THE INVENTOR
OF THE TELEPHONE,
COULDN'T CALL HIS WIFE...
SHE WAS DEAF

GETH WOULD LIKE TO THANK PETE

PETE WOULD LIKE TO THANK GETH

AND WE WOULD BOTH LIKE TO
THANK EVERYONE THAT HAS
HELPED ALONG THE WAY...

"LEARN SOMETHING EVERY DAY" IS A SELF-INITIATED PROJECT
BY YOUNG. YOUNG IS A CREATIVE AGENCY BASED IN THE U.K.
FOUNDED BY PETER JARVIS AND GETHIN VAUGHAN.
WWW. LEARN SOMETHINGEVERYDAY.CO.UK
WWW. WEARE YOUNG.CO.UK